POSITIVE PSYCHOLOGY FOR A POSITIVE LIFE

7 Psychological Ways to Overcome Overthinking and Regain Mental Clarity

Ram Prudhvi Teja

The author of this book does not recommend medical advice or prescribe the use of any technique as a form of treatment for physical or psychological problems. This book provides general insights to guide you toward positive well-being. Should you choose to apply any of the concepts shared within these pages, you do so at your discretion. The author and publisher bear no responsibility for the choices you make along the way.

First Edition

Dedicated to my guru,

Ibraahim Mohammad.

ACKNOWLEDGMENT

Writing a book is always a tough challenge, and it would not have been possible without the love and support of those who care about me and encourage me to pursue my dreams in all aspects of my life. My accomplishments, rewards, and overall success would not have been possible without the help of the people mentioned below.

There are no words to adequately express my gratitude to you, Amma (Smt. Jyothi), for your love and support. You made me what I am today. Words fail me when it comes to expressing my gratitude for your unwavering love and support in all parts of my life. I am forever indebted to you for your unconditional love.

You are always my inspiration, Dad (Sri. Satyanarayana). Your morals and teachings have shaped my personality. You are my role model. Thank you so much for your encouragement and unwavering support throughout the years.

I am so grateful to my guru, Ibrahim Mohammad (late), for his guidance and teachings. His invaluable life lessons have significantly impacted my life, and I am sincerely missing you, sir. Thank you so much for introducing the world of psychology to me.

I am blessed to have my brothers, Aditya Teja and Manoj Teja, as the two pillars of my strength. Thank you both for supporting and loving me endlessly. I also wish to thank my in-laws, Smt. Sowjanya and Smt. Prasanna, for your help and care!

Thank you to my dearest friends for being my staunchest supporters throughout my literary career.

I want to thank my global family on Facebook and Instagram for investing time and money in reading my work. Writers cannot exist without readers, and I sincerely appreciate their support.

Table of Contents

INTRODUCTION

Have you ever observed a buffalo bringing up food from its stomach and then spending time ruminating on it? Similarly, people tend to take their problems into their minds and begin ruminating on them, leading to mental, physical, and emotional exhaustion by the end of the day. As a psychologist, I understand that a certain level of rational and conscious thinking is necessary for problem-solving; however, too much thinking can be detrimental. In fact, overthinking is a major contributor to mental stress, as it heightens alertness and triggers the release of the stress hormone **cortisol**. Even scientific studies show that excessive cortisol production can weaken the immune system and negatively impact physical health. In some cases, it may even lead to both psychological and physical illnesses.

Let's understand what overthinking is in simple terms. Overthinking, or rumination, occurs when your mind repeatedly processes thoughts about past or future events or problems in an endless loop. This can lead to your mind operating in a default mode in which your thoughts, emotions, and behaviors become automatic, much like a computer program running beyond your conscious control. Overthinking can have several negative impacts on your life. First, it can drain your energy and leave you mentally exhausted, affecting your productivity and overall well-being. Second, it can cause you to miss the present moment and lose touch with your surroundings. Third, it can trigger feelings of anxiety, stress, and even depression, along with other mental and physical health problems.

Overthinking is a common psychological problem. In fact, research studies show that more than 73% of adults in the age range of 25–35 are found to be chronic overthinkers, along with 52% of people ages 35–55. Overthinking is a mental act in which a person thinks about something for an extended period and becomes trapped in the vicious cycle of thought patterns that one struggles to break free from. In this book, you will learn some evidence-based psychological techniques that can help overcome overthinking.

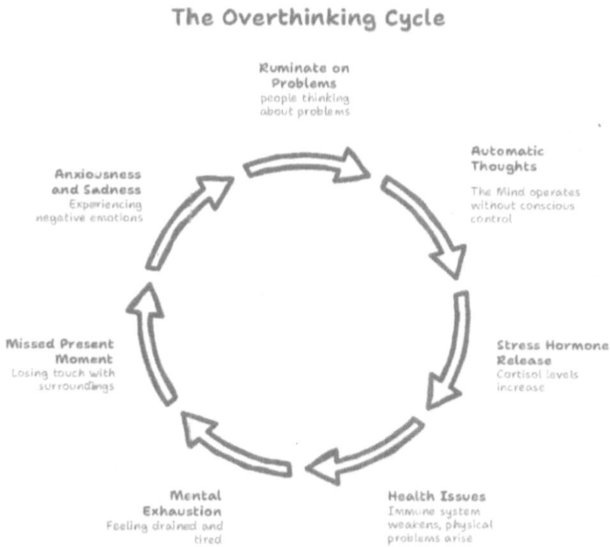

First, let's understand some of the primary signs and symptoms of overthinking.

1. Analysis Paralysis: In general, we make many decisions daily. However, we spend some extra time and effort to make an important decision, which is quite common, but when it comes to overthinkers, they spend all of their mental energy and time finding out all possible options to make the finest and best decision, even for a small, trivial thing, due to excessive worry of making a wrong decision or fear of being judged. These people are typically trapped in an endless loop of "*what if that*" scenarios, and they eventually become so overwhelmed that they fail to make any decisions. This is due to a false sense of perfectionism or fear of failure that develops in the early stages of life.

2. Mind—Fullness: Clinical overthinkers frequently spend their time either reliving past memories—experiencing shame, guilt, and sadness—or anticipating worst-case scenarios about future events—feeling anxious and worried. This vicious cycle of moving back and forth between the past and the future causes them to live in a state of hopelessness, where unconscious overthinking processes consume their time and energy. One way to better understand this is to imagine being lost in your own thoughts, trapped in a repetitive mental loop that prevents you from fully engaging with the present moment.

3. Deprivation of sleep: Overthinking tends to be more active at night, just before bedtime, because your brain and body are in rest mode, free from mental/physical tasks and distractions. With fewer external stimuli, your mind is more likely to wander between past regrets and future worries, leading to excessive analysis. This continuous stream of thoughts can make it difficult to relax and fall asleep, potentially resulting in long-term sleep disturbances. In some cases, it can also lead to insomnia or sleep disorders.

4. Mind-readers: Our brains are inherently designed to keep us safe and constantly attempt to protect us from the outside world's threats. So, it is always looking for patterns and combinations in the brain to make guesses about future events or people based on past experiences. For instance, because you had a bad breakup in the past, you are convinced that men will cheat on you in the name of love. A previous lousy breakup does not guarantee that you will experience another. However, you use that past experience as evidence for your belief, drawing conclusions and making assumptions. As a result, you will avoid meeting new people, and if you do have the chance to meet new people or go on a date, you will assume that this man will also cheat on you.

Overthinkers are highly prone to believing in and acting upon their irrational thoughts and assumptions, which reinforces their beliefs and creates a self-perpetuating cycle of overanalysis and emotional distress. It's essential to understand that your thoughts and perceptions are deeply influenced by past experiences. The beliefs, schemas, and mental models you have developed subconsciously shape how you perceive yourself and others around you. As a result, you may unknowingly filter reality through the lens of negative beliefs accumulated over the years, further fueling overthinking.

5. Procrastination: People who overthink may have difficulty making decisions and taking action. This tendency to overanalyze frequently leads to procrastination as they struggle to decide. They may spend a significant amount of time exploring and evaluating various options, attempting to weigh the benefits and drawbacks of each. This lengthy and intensive evaluation process can result in analysis paralysis, in which the individual becomes stuck and unable to decide. As a result, overthinkers may experience anxiety and stress as they obsess over every possible scenario, delaying action or making a decision entirely. This cycle can be exhausting and frustrating, leaving them mentally and physically exhausted.

In the next section, you can find some evidence-based psychological strategies to help you manage overthinking and regain mental clarity.

These are some of the primary signs and symptoms of overthinking. Now, let's understand why people get stuck in this pattern and what the underlying reasons might be. The following are some of the core factors that act as root causes of overthinking.

1. False Sense of Control: One of the primary reasons for overthinking is the belief that analyzing a situation in depth will grant complete control over it, causing the brain to switch into "*analysis mode.*" People who struggle with overthinking often have the irrational belief that they should be able to control everything that happens in their lives. As a result, they spend excessive time ruminating on the same thoughts or situations.

2. A false sense of perfectionism: At some point in my life, I struggled with this false perfectionism, the irrational belief that I needed to be perfect at what I did to meet other people's expectations. Thus, the combination of perfectionism and fear of rejection pushed me out of my limits, which threw me into a state of overthinking for many years.

3. False sense of belief: Your beliefs shape your thoughts, and your thoughts serve as the lens through which you perceive the world. Suppose you hold irrational (baseless or illogical) beliefs about yourself, others, and the future. In that case, you tend to think, feel, and act within the limitations of those beliefs, making it difficult to perceive the world beyond those self-limited beliefs. For example, suppose you believe and surrender to the irrational thought (intermediate belief) that *"nobody loves me because I am a failure, and I know my future will be a mess"* because it is anchored and rooted in your subconscious mind. In that case, this irrational belief about yourself, others, and your future will never allow you to think, feel, or act beyond it. This way of thinking can also be the root cause of overthinking.

4. False sense of reassurance: People who experience obsessive thoughts or chronic overthinking tend to develop a habit of seeking mental reassurance, also known as a compulsive mental act. They become addicted to reassurance, believing they can control every possible outcome by thinking over and over again. Subconsciously, they may feel that analyzing problems in greater depth will help solve them. Still, their thoughts grow stronger each time they seek reassurance, reigniting their intensity.

They become trapped in this cycle because they believe that meticulously planning every detail will help them achieve perfection, avoid mistakes, and eliminate uncertainty. In some cases, overthinkers seek reassurance from others by asking endless questions that arise in their minds. Through this process, they unconsciously become attached to their stream of thoughts, making reassurance-seeking a difficult habit to break. Over time, this pattern turns into a coping mechanism—one they rely on to avoid fear and temporarily soothe distressing thoughts, even though it ultimately reinforces and sustains the cycle of overthinking.

5. Trauma or past experiences: Trauma survivors may develop hypervigilance, meaning they are constantly on high alert, with their stress response always activated. They pay close attention to everything around them, often analyzing situations in detail to predict potential threats. As a result, overthinking can become a coping mechanism—a way to regain a sense of control. By mentally running through every possible scenario, they may feel more prepared to handle whatever comes their way. However, this heightened awareness elevates stress levels, significantly impacting their thought patterns.

Ultimately, past trauma and experiences can lead people to overthink as a means of managing distress and regaining control over their lives. Yet, this habit often becomes counterproductive, increasing anxiety and stress rather than providing relief.

Overthinking can be harmful when it becomes a persistent habit since unhealthy thoughts lead to unhealthy feelings and unhealthy behavior, which can have negative consequences for both physical and mental health. Some of the most common health consequences are the following:

1. Anxiety: One of the most common consequences of overthinking is anxiety. Overthinking can lead to heightened stress levels, which can cause anxiety attacks, social anxiety, and other anxiety-related disorders. As an individual continues to overthink, they may become trapped in a cycle of anxious thoughts and feelings, which can worsen over time.

2. Depression: In addition to anxiety, overthinking can also contribute to depression. When individuals become overwhelmed by negative thoughts and emotions, they may experience persistent low moods, loss of interest in activities they once enjoyed, sleep disturbances, difficulty concentrating, fatigue, and a decrease in libido. Over time, this cycle can lead to clinical depression, which, in some cases, may require help from a mental health professional.

3. Relationship: Overthinking can also impact relationships, mainly if one constantly analyzes and second-guesses their partner's actions. This can lead to a strained relationship where communication breaks down and trust is lost.

4. Productivity: Furthermore, overthinking can reduce productivity and make it difficult to focus on tasks. People may become distracted and lose motivation to complete tasks, leading to decreased efficiency and quality of work.

5. Physical Health: Finally, too much thinking can hurt your body, like headaches, muscle tension, stomach issues, and psychosomatic problems. As the body remains in a state of stress for prolonged periods, it can lead to chronic health issues that require medical attention.

7 PSYCHOLOGICAL WAYS TO OVERCOME OVERTHINKING

Overthinking can be challenging to break, especially when it has become deeply ingrained in your thought patterns. However, it is not impossible to overcome. Remember, overcoming overthinking requires time, patience, and consistent effort. It's important to be kind to yourself throughout the process, understanding that change doesn't happen overnight. With consistency and persistence, you can cultivate a more balanced mindset and break the cycle of overthinking.

1

IDENTIFY YOUR ENEMY (DESTRUCTIVE THOUGHT PATTERN)

"Overthinking is the enemy of happiness; it can lead to anxiety, stress, and depression."

--Unknown

Overthinking is the tendency to dwell excessively on a situation or problem, making it difficult to make decisions or take action. It can be frustrating because the more you analyze a problem, the more stressed and overwhelmed you may feel. Additionally, overthinking can trap you in a cycle of repetitive thoughts, as unconscious thinking patterns tend to reinforce themselves over time.

The first step in overcoming overthinking is recognizing when you're caught in an unhelpful or destructive thought pattern. This can be challenging, as many people may not even realize they are overthinking. However, by paying close attention to your thoughts and emotions, you can identify when you are stuck in a cycle of rumination. Once you become aware of your overthinking, exploring why it's happening is essential. Understanding the root cause can help you break the habit more effectively. Overthinking can stem from various factors, including stress, fear, anxiety, uncertainty, habitual overanalysis, or the causes mentioned above in this book—*factors that influence your thoughts in the background.*

By identifying what triggers your overthinking and how it impacts your life, you can apply the psychological strategies and techniques learned in this book to regain control over your thoughts and develop a healthier mindset.

Thinking about things too much all the time can be tiring and harmful to your mental health. Practicing mindfulness is an effective strategy to help overcome this thinking pattern. At its core, mindfulness is about being present in the moment and paying attention to your thoughts and emotions without judgment. By doing so, you can become more aware of your thought patterns and be better equipped to overcome them. Mindfulness involves focusing on the present moment, noticing any thoughts or feelings that arise, and observing them without judgment *(not assigning any meaning to your thoughts).* This means that instead of getting caught up in the content of your thoughts, you simply observe them as they come and go. Thoughts are like water flowing in a river. When you dwell on them, they become stuck in your mind, leading to overthinking. However, by practicing mindfulness and simply observing your thoughts, you allow them to continue flowing naturally. With regular practice, mindfulness can help you develop a greater awareness of your thought patterns and help you recognize when you are overthinking. You can cultivate a greater sense of presence, reduce anxiety, and improve your overall mental well-being through mindfulness.

Suppose you're interested in learning more about mindfulness and how to practice it. In that case, various resources are available, including books, courses, and mindfulness apps. Moreover, in the next section of this book, you can learn more about mindfulness and how to practice it in detail.

2

MINDFULNESS

"Mindfulness is the antidote to overthinking." It allows us to step back and observe our thoughts without getting lost

—Kristin Neff

Mindfulness is a mental practice in which an individual trains their mind to become aware of their thoughts, emotions, words, behaviors, and physical sensations. Through mindfulness exercises, a person intentionally focuses on the present moment without judgment rather than becoming unconsciously entangled in automatic or ruminative thoughts.

Practicing **mindfulness** teaches one to detach from one's thoughts, observing them from a distance rather than identifying with them. This shift allows the individual to develop greater self-awareness and emotional regulation. In contrast, when a person experiences **mind-fullness,** they remain subconsciously immersed in their thoughts, becoming absorbed in an endless stream of overanalysis and mental chattering. Instead of observing their thoughts, they react to them automatically and become absorbed in their never-ending thoughts.

The fundamental nature of the mind is to operate within the confines of what it has learned, experienced, or accumulated over time. It relies on past knowledge, memories, and acquired information to process thoughts, analyze situations, and make decisions. As a result, the mind tends to dwell between past experiences and future possibilities, often replaying previous events or projecting potential outcomes. This continuous back-and-forth movement between past and future shapes perceptions, emotions, and responses, making it challenging to remain fully present in the moment. When you are not fully engaged in the present moment, your memories of the past or anticipation of the future can influence your thoughts and emotions, leading to overthinking or rumination.

Being present at the moment means focusing on what is happening, while mindfulness is the intentional practice of observing your thoughts, emotions, and surroundings without judgment. The best way to manage overthinking is to develop mindfulness, which involves becoming more conscious of your unconscious thought patterns. If your mind wanders, practicing mindfulness helps gently bring your attention back with awareness.

Each time you engage in mindfulness, you are actively training or signaling your mind to observe thoughts without attachment, reducing the emotional impact of past experiences. This heightened awareness lets you understand your thoughts, feelings, and behaviors more clearly. Integrating mindfulness into your daily life allows you to make better decisions and respond to situations more clearly, rather than being driven by habitual thought patterns.

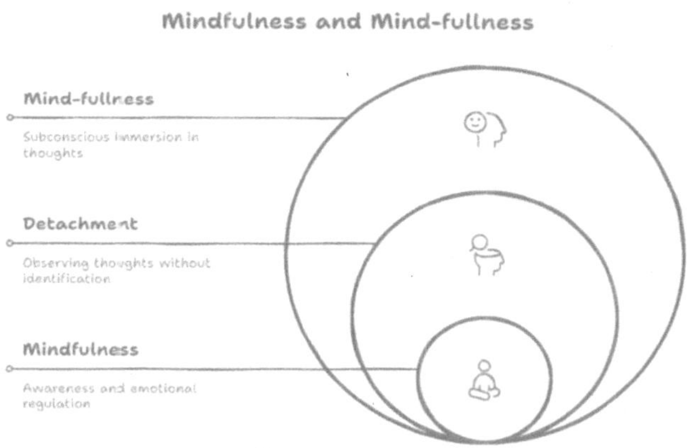

One of the better ways to practice mindfulness is

Walking Meditation:

For most of your day, you operate from your subconscious programs, which you unconsciously act upon. For instance, while having your meal, you are watching television; on the other hand, you are chitchatting with your friend. You unconsciously operate three activities or programs simultaneously—*watching, chatting, and eating*. From a neuroscience point of view, multitasking can also be the primary cause of overthinking since it primarily impacts your neocortex, which means your thinking brain, which runs on different programs simultaneously. In a way, you are putting too much weight on your brain, which it cannot handle for prolonged periods.

You may already be familiar with sitting meditation, which you may have heard many times before. However, in this book, you will learn about walking meditation and how to practice it to improve the quality of being in the present moment. This helps reduce stress, anxiety, sadness, and overthinking by turning off the default mode (unconscious thought process).

Walking meditation is a form of mindfulness meditation that blends mind-body connectivity; it is widely practiced by Buddhist monks and is also well-known as "**Kinhin meditation**." Unlike traditional sitting meditation, walking meditation is typically performed with eyes open, allowing practitioners to engage more fully with their body movements, specific hand postures, and sensations.

HOW TO PRACTICE WALKING MEDITATION STEP BY STEP

Step 1: When you first begin practicing walking meditation, finding a quiet place in nature where you won't be disturbed or distracted is the best way of practicing it in your beginning days. You can even do it in crowded places once you've mastered it. While doing walking meditation, I encourage you not to pay attention to anything or anyone outside of yourself for the next couple of minutes. Instead, let yourself be wholly present and focus on your inner self. (*I am asking you to disconnect from things and objects in your surroundings.*)

Step 2: Begin your walking meditation by gradually focusing on your in-breath and out-breath as you take slow, steady steps along the path (ground). The mind is often compared to a monkey's mind because it constantly jumps from one thought to another, pulling you away from the present moment. If your mind wanders or drifts into unconscious thoughts, gently guide your attention back to your breathing without frustration or judgment. Accept that distraction is a natural tendency of the mind. All you need to do is return your focus to the present moment and reconnect with your breath. Remember, the more you practice mindfulness, the better you manage rumination. With each moment of awareness, you train yourself to be more mindful, gradually weakening the grip of overthinking and restoring clarity to your mind.

Remember that when you bring your attention back to the present moment while your mind drifts to the past or future, you are repairing a portion of your overthinking and weakening the power of the emotions attached to your ruminative thoughts. In other words, you are simply lowering the volume of your ruminative thoughts.

Step 3: After 5–10 minutes of focusing on your breathing, focus on your body movements, concentrating on each step—lifting and placing your feet on the ground—while paying close attention to your body's movements and sensations. By sustaining your presence in the moment for an extended period through walking meditation, you can enhance your ability to observe your thoughts rather than unconsciously becoming entangled. As you practice walking meditation, be open to noticing changes within yourself, moving forward from past unconscious patterns to your entire presence with each step you take.

Walking meditation aims to close the doors of your past unconscious programs and your ruminative thinking, which run day in and day out, and stay in the present moment. The beauty of staying in the present moment is that you can use your mental energy to create your life as a creator instead of living as a victim of your past unconscious thoughts. The more you practice walking meditation, the more likely you are to change your state of mind.

ACT AS IF YOU ARE A "DIRECTOR":

Another powerful mindfulness exercise to stop overthinking is observing your thoughts rather than getting lost in them. Overthinking often leads to a constant stream of analysis, which can feel overwhelming and mentally exhausting. To break this cycle, you must step back and become an observer of your thoughts. Observing your thoughts means watching them without judgment from a place of detachment. This shift in perspective allows you to see your thoughts more objectively and recognize patterns that may include negative or limiting beliefs.

THE ART OF OBSERVING

To become an observer of your thoughts, you must first develop awareness. Pay attention to the thoughts running through your mind and notice when you get caught up in them. Practice detachment once you recognize these thoughts—watch them without becoming emotionally involved.

One effective way to cultivate detachment is to imagine yourself sitting in a movie theater, watching your thoughts appear on a screen before you. Instead of getting absorbed in the storyline of your thoughts, observe them from a distance, as if you were watching a film. Avoid resisting or reacting to them; watch them as a neutral observer and let them pass. Each time you do this, you lessen the emotional intensity attached to your thoughts. Over time, practicing the art of observation helps break the mental habit of overthinking.

For example, imagine you have sent an important message to someone at work, and you have not received a response yet. Soon, your mind begins to fill with thoughts such as, *"Did I say something wrong?"*, *"What if they are upset with me?"*, or *"This could affect my job."* As these thoughts arise, your anxiety starts to increase, and you feel restless and distracted.

Instead of getting caught in this stream of thoughts, you pause and shift into the role of an observer. You imagine yourself sitting in a movie theater, watching these thoughts appear on a screen. One thought shows up: *"I might have made a mistake."* Another follows: *"This situation could go badly."* Rather than reacting to them or trying to push them away, you simply notice them—*"This is a worried thought,"* or *"This is a fear-based assumption."*

You do not argue with the thoughts, nor do you follow them further. You watch them come and go, just as scenes in a movie change. As you observe without judgment, the emotional intensity begins to settle. Your body relaxes, and your mind feels less crowded. By stepping back and observing, you recognize that these thoughts are not facts—they are mental events. From this calmer, more objective space, you can choose how to respond rather than react. You may decide to wait for a reply, focus on your current task, or remind yourself that silence does not automatically mean something negative.

This is the art of observing: *learning to watch your thoughts without becoming entangled in them.* With regular practice, this skill helps weaken overthinking and strengthens your ability to remain present, balanced, and emotionally resilient.

It's important to remember that becoming an observer of your thoughts is a skill that takes time to develop. You won't master it overnight, but it becomes easier with patience and consistent practice. The more you engage in this practice, the greater the benefits you will experience.

The key difference between mindfulness and becoming an observer is that mindfulness involves simply being aware of and accepting your thoughts without judgment—**focusing on awareness and acceptance**. In contrast, becoming an observer (or director) requires actively stepping back, analyzing your thoughts objectively, and consciously deciding how to frame or reshape the narrative—**changing your perspective on the storyline of your thoughts.**

Remember, becoming an observer of your thoughts is a lifelong journey. The more you practice, the easier it becomes to detach from overthinking and move toward a balanced, fulfilling life.

3

FIX YOUR THINKING ERRORS

"Cognitive distortions are like a pair of glasses that we wear, shaping our perception of reality." Overthinking only strengthens their grip.

- Unknown

Cognitive distortions, also known as mental or thinking errors, are patterns of thinking that can lead you to misinterpret reality. These thought patterns can be harmful and irrational, causing you to see situations in life as more complicated than they really are. If you view the world through the lens of cognitive distortions, your thoughts may twist your reality, leading you to believe things that are not actually true. In other words, cognitive distortions refer to a biased and irrational way of looking at things in life, which can impact your perceptions, emotions, thoughts, and actions. Cognitive distortions are how your mind convinces you of something that isn't necessarily true, but you believe it to be true.

An example of cognitive distortion is when you think your husband no longer loves you, which is an irrational or faulty thought. This thought may arise when you notice that your husband is no longer showing as much care or spending as much quality time with you as he used to. When these kinds of thoughts come up, they can lead to a chain of negative or irrational thoughts that support the first idea or thought. This can lead to a never-ending loop of excessive rumination.

As you keep believing these irrational thoughts to be true, your view of reality can become skewed, and you may start looking for signs or evidence that back up your assumptions and beliefs. For instance, you may start thinking that your husband no longer loves you because he has lost interest in you or is having an affair with someone else. Suppose you hold onto such irrational beliefs and assumptions. In that case, your mind will likely focus on finding evidence to support them, leading you to focus on your husband's faults and justifications instead of seeing the other side of the story.

It is important to remember that one negative or dysfunctional thought can lead to another, creating a cycle of overthinking that reinforces negative thought patterns (it *all starts with a single thought that you believe to be true*). This can be difficult to break because it triggers unhealthy emotions and unhelpful actions.

Let's explore some of the cognitive distortions that are commonly associated with overthinking:

All-or-nothing thinking, also called polarized thinking: This distortion involves viewing a situation in terms of extremes. For instance, thinking, *"Either my husband is innocent or a ruthless cheater."*

Catastrophizing: This distortion predicts a negative outcome without considering alternative possibilities. An example would be saying, *"I know my husband is going to divorce me."*

Overgeneralization: This distortion involves drawing conclusions that are not supported by evidence. An example would be thinking, *"My husband never cares about me anymore."*

Mental filtering: This distortion refers to selectively focusing on negative details while failing to see the big picture. It means seeing only one side of a situation, usually the negative one. An example of this would be assuming, *"My husband always comes home late because he is spending time with his new girlfriend."*

Emotional reasoning: This distortion believes something is true because it feels true. It is the belief that one's feelings accurately reflect reality. An example would be saying, *"I'm feeling depressed because I'm in a toxic relationship."*

Cognitive restructuring is a cognitive behavioral therapy (CBT) technique that changes dysfunctional thinking patterns and fixes cognitive distortions.

Here's a step-by-step process for modifying your cognitive distortions:

Step 1: Self-monitoring: The first step involves recognizing your cognitive distortions, which are the underlying cause of maladaptive or overthinking patterns. Understanding your thinking patterns, the statements you make to yourself and others, and the actions you take in response to your thoughts are the first steps in recognizing cognitive distortions.

Cognitive restructuring relies on your ability to identify and analyze unhealthy thoughts. Keeping a thought diary or journaling can be helpful for some individuals. Even if you're uncertain about what's causing your overthinking, anxiety, or sadness, writing down your thoughts may help you pinpoint a cognitive distortion or negative thought pattern.

Step 2: Examine and dispute your dysfunctional thoughts: Socratic questioning is a well-known technique in cognitive restructuring that helps to evaluate and discover false thoughts and beliefs and raise awareness through the disciplined practice of thoughtful questioning.

Here are a few examples of questions that can be asked using the Socratic method:

1. What evidence supports this thought or belief?
2. Am I basing this thought on facts or feelings?
3. Are there any alternative explanations for this thought or situation?

By asking these questions, you can better understand your distorted beliefs or dysfunctional thoughts and work towards developing clarity and rational thinking.

Step 3: Replacing or altering your thoughts: Once you have identified and evaluated your cognitive distortions, it is time to transform your irrational thinking into more rational thinking. This step involves finding alternative thoughts to your current dysfunctional ones that are more valid and helpful to you. The goal is to alter your unhealthy thought process to a healthy one and change your perceptions (how you view the situation) through cognitive restructuring.

For instance:

Instead of thinking, "*My husband always comes home late because he is spending time with his new girlfriend*," you could think, "*My husband sometimes comes home late because he may have worked at the office, and he works hard for our family.*"

Instead of thinking, "*I know my husband is going to divorce me*," you could think, *"My marriage is stronger than I thought. We have issues but are committed to our marriage and willing to work through them."*

Instead of thinking, *"I am feeling depressed because I'm in a toxic relationship,"* you could think, *"I need to evaluate my relationship and determine what changes we can make to improve it."*

It is important to remember that emotional reactions are not caused by the situation per se but by your interpretations and beliefs. How you perceive an event shapes your thoughts, feelings, and behavior, ultimately influencing the outcome. The primary goal of cognitive restructuring is to identify, evaluate, and modify dysfunctional thoughts and beliefs that contribute to overthinking. You can develop a healthier and more balanced mindset by challenging and reframing these negative thought patterns.

Pause for a second and question yourself gently, *"Which thinking error might be influencing the way I am seeing my distress situation or the way I am thinking?"*

4

CLEAN YOUR TRASH

> *"Overthinking about past traumatic experiences is like revisiting a prison that you've already been released from." It only serves to keep you trapped.*
>
> *- Unknown*

Overthinking can be triggered by various factors; past experiences or traumatic events are often significant contributing factors. It can usually cause individuals to replay scenarios and dwell on the negative feelings associated with those events. Forming mental patterns is one of the main ways previous experiences are associated with overthinking. Our brains naturally seek patterns and make connections between different pieces of information, which can be helpful in many situations. But when bad things happen, or you feel sad, your brain can create patterns that make you overthink. For example, if someone has experienced rejection, they may believe that they will always be rejected and start to overthink every social interaction as a potential rejection. This thought pattern can be challenging to break, leading to significant stress and anxiety.

Another way in which past experiences can contribute to overthinking is through the activation of emotional triggers. When you experience a traumatic event, your brain can create strong emotional associations with specific triggers that are present during the event. For example, someone in a car accident might feel too worried when they see a car approaching too fast or hear brakes screeching. This kind of trigger can be hard to get past, which can cause a lot of worry and anxiety.

Past experiences or traumatic events can also impact your beliefs and values, contributing to overthinking. For example, suppose someone grew up in an environment where they were constantly criticized or punished for making mistakes. In that case, they may believe they must always be perfect to avoid punishment. This belief can lead to overthinking and excessive worry about making mistakes or failing in any way. (*A sense of false perfectionism*).

The impact of constantly dwelling on past negative thoughts and scenarios can not only significantly affect an individual's mental health, relationships, and quality of life, but it also leads to anxiety, depression, and other mental health issues.

You can learn and apply strategies or techniques to detach yourself from past ruminating thoughts that cause overthinking.

1. Reframe your thoughts: One way to let go of the past is to reframe your thoughts about the situation. Reframing involves looking at an experience from a different perspective and finding a more positive or constructive meaning. For example, suppose you have experienced a traumatic event. In that case, you can reframe your thoughts by focusing on how you overcame and grew stronger. By reframing your thoughts, you can change your perception of your past storyline, allowing you to release negative emotions and shift your focus toward the positive aspects of your experiences.

For instance, imagine someone who was criticized repeatedly by a supervisor in the past. Each time he recalls this experience, he feels inadequate and discouraged. By reframing the memory, he begins to view it differently—not as proof of failure, but as a phase that helped him recognize his strengths, improve his skills, and develop resilience. Instead of thinking, *"I wasn't good enough,"* he shifts to, *"That experience helped me grow and become more capable."*

By changing how the experience is interpreted, the emotional weight attached to the memory gradually reduces, allowing the person to move forward with greater confidence and emotional freedom. By altering how you view your past experiences, you can effectively transform the emotional patterns associated with those memories. Remember that liberation from your past begins if you can detach emotion from a memory. This shift enables you to overcome repetitive thoughts and ruminations, leading to a sense of emotional freedom. It's essential to recognize that memories are not objective; your interpretation of events is subjective. This means your perceptions influence your emotions and reactions to those memories. Changing your perceptions can reshape how you feel about the past. Identifying and reframing your perceptions allows you to live more fully and peacefully in the present rather than being weighed down by past experiences.

2. Practice Forgiveness: Forgiveness is a powerful tool for letting go of the past. Holding onto grudges and resentment can prevent you from moving on and cause you to overthink past events. By practicing forgiveness, you can release negative emotions and move forward. Forgiveness does not mean forgetting what happened or condoning the behavior of others. Instead, it means acknowledging what happened and letting go of the negative feelings associated with the event. By forgiving yourself and others, you can free yourself from the emotional baggage weighing you down. *Forgiveness is the best medicine to release your past unhealthy emotions.*

The Exercise of Forgiveness

Sit or lie down in a comfortable chair or on the bed. Please close your eyes (make sure to do this exercise in a dark room or a place where no daylight or room light enters your eyes so your brain waves get lower into the theta state). For the following three to five minutes, focus on your inhalation and exhalation *(in-breath and out-breath*). Allow your respiration to be free to calm your mind and body. If past memories provoke this practice, simply let them go and refocus your attention on your breathing.

Then, visualize the person that you want to forgive. Bring him or her to your attention. (*Imagine this with your mind's eye.*) Imagine that you are viewing that person standing in front of you. Now, it's time to forgive that person by expressing your forgiveness to him or her.

Example: I heartfully forgive you, Rahul, for spreading rumors about me in our class, and I fully accept the wrongdoing you committed against me. I choose to release any lingering resentment and anger from my heart, understanding that holding onto these feelings only weighs me down. I recognize that we all make mistakes, and I acknowledge your actions without minimizing the hurt they caused.

By letting go of the past, I free myself to move forward with compassion and peace. I wish you clarity and growth, and I hope that you, too, can learn and become better from this experience. From this moment on, I release the negative emotions attached to this incident. I reclaim my sense of self-worth and inner calm. May healing and understanding flourish between us, allowing both of us to find closure and wisdom.

I am grateful for the strength I have found in choosing forgiveness, and I welcome harmony—within myself and in my interactions with others. Practice this forgiveness exercise for one person at a time.

Affirming this statement is associated with the feeling of forgiveness (empathy and compassion) in your heart, which connects directly with your subconscious mind. Use the above example to create or prepare your statements/affirmations.

Forgiveness is not only for other people. It can also be used to forgive yourself to relieve shame, guilt, regrets, and other self-harming unpleasant feelings. So, practice self-forgiveness exercises on yourself as well.

Remember that forgiving is an inward process (inside job) that takes considerable time. If you only do this exercise once, you will never be able to forgive someone who has done something terrible or has badly harmed you. You must repeat this activity regularly to detach yourself from that emotional baggage. After weeks of practicing forgiveness, you will notice a significant shift in your thoughts and emotional patterns. I understand how difficult it is to forgive someone who has done you wrong, but forgiveness is about YOU, not others. However, you can only experience peace, happiness, and liberation when you release the heavy baggage you've been carrying for ages. I am sure that no circumstances, triggers, or person will ever let you down if you start practicing this forgiveness exercise or 'let it go' method. When it comes to having a good and happy life, forgiveness is an essential component.

The following are some of the advantages of practicing forgiveness:

- It enhances the quality of your positive thoughts.
- It enriches your overall sense of well-being.
- It promotes healing for both the mind and body.
- It helps you move forward toward fulfilling your desires.
- It strengthens your intuition and self-awareness.

3. Create new experiences: Another method for letting go of your past is to break your habitual thinking patterns by engaging in new activities and experiences to shift your focus away from past events and create new positive memories. This can help you break the cycle of overthinking and move forward with your life. Consider trying new engagement activities, such as learning a new skill, hitting the gym, playing the sport you love, attending a music class, enrolling in a course, getting into creative artwork, or traveling to a new place. By stepping out of your comfort zone and exploring new experiences, you can gain a new perspective on life and let go of past events. In fact, more than 90% of your thoughts today are the same as they were yesterday.

Focusing all your attention on your past memories keeps you thinking about the same thoughts and performing the same routine habits that create your present reality based on your past experiences. Therefore, you make the same reality you have previously experienced (recreating the familiar past). Remember, creating new experiences and memories is not about erasing the past or denying its existence; instead, it is about taking control of your life and focusing on the present. So, go ahead and try something new today—*you never know what wonderful memories it may bring!*

Pause for a second and question yourself gently, *"Is there a person or an event from your past that you still need to heal from?*

5

CATCH THAT FISH

> *"The more we overthink, the more we feed our fears, and the more we feed our fears, the more we overthink. It's a vicious cycle."*
>
> *- Unknown.*

Fear is a natural primary human emotion, but it can become a significant challenge when it becomes overwhelming and disrupts daily life. Overthinking involves obsessive analysis and reanalysis of situations or events, often fueled by worry and fear. It creates a cycle of negative thoughts that can lead to various problems.

One primary way overthinking relates to fear is through forming negative thought patterns. Overthinkers tend to dwell on negative scenarios and outcomes, frequently imagining worst-case situations that are unlikely to happen in the future. This pattern of thinking heightens fear and anxiety as individuals become fixated on potential dangers and risks. For example, someone overthinking an upcoming job interview may repeatedly envision failure or embarrassment, intensifying their fear and anxiety about the event.

Overthinking or rumination can also trigger fear by activating the body's stress response. When you experience fear, your fight-or-flight response is triggered, preparing you to confront or escape a perceived threat. However, overthinking can activate this response without real danger (an imaginary threat), leading to physical symptoms such as an increased heart rate, sweating, and muscle tension. These symptoms, in turn, can intensify fear and anxiety, creating a vicious cycle of overthinking and fear. Additionally, fear reinforces overthinking by strengthening negative thought patterns. When you experience fear, your brain forms strong emotional associations with the triggers that caused it. For instance, someone who fears public speaking may repeatedly imagine worst-case scenarios, such as forgetting their lines or being ridiculed by the audience. As a result, they may either avoid public speaking altogether (avoidance behavior) or experience excessive anxiety and stress when faced with such situations. This pattern creates a negative feedback loop where the fear of public speaking fuels overthinking, which, in turn, intensifies fear and anxiety.

Here's a step-by-step process for eliminating the fear:

1. Identify the root cause of your fear: The first step in overcoming overthinking by addressing fear is identifying its root cause. Ask yourself what is triggering your overthinking and fear. Gaining clarity on the underlying issues can help you develop a strategy to manage them effectively. For example, if you constantly worry about your job performance, consider the core reason behind this fear. *Are you afraid of being fired? Are you anxious about shifting into a new job role?* Once you pinpoint the root cause, you can take proactive steps to address it.

2. Challenge your thoughts: After identifying the root cause of your overthinking, the next step is to challenge your thoughts. Negative self-talk and irrational beliefs are often the culprits behind excessive ruminating. By challenging these thoughts, you can break the cycle of overthinking and alleviate anxiety.

For instance, if you discover that your fear stems from the possibility of being fired, you can start challenging this thought by asking yourself some questions. For example, "*What evidence do I have that I will be fired?*" or "*Is there a possibility that my assumptions are incorrect?*" By questioning your thoughts, you can view them more objectively and reduce their hold on you.

Not all thoughts are facts. Your mind always makes stuff up. So, instead of believing whatever thoughts come to your mind, it's a better practice to challenge them so that you can start to break the cycle of overthinking and gain a new perspective on your thoughts and beliefs. This mental exercise can help you make better decisions, reduce stress and anxiety, and improve your overall well-being.

It's important to note that challenging negative thoughts may be difficult initially. However, you can gradually weaken their power and gain control over them with practice. Additionally, it's crucial to replace negative self-talk with more positive and realistic statements (positive self-talk). This can help counteract the effects of overthinking.

3. Take action: The most effective way to overcome fear is through gradual exposure. Taking action empowers you to regain control of your situation and reduce anxiety. If fear or uncertainty feels overwhelming, start by identifying a small step you can take to address the issue and begin moving forward. Avoidance may provide temporary relief, but in the long run, it reinforces fear, making it even more potent. On the other hand, by gradually facing your fears through exposure, you can build resilience and eventually overcome them.

For instance, if you're worried about being fired or your job performance, you can take a small step by working on your skills and knowledge in your relevant field. Committing to continuous learning and updating industry trends can boost your confidence and improve your performance. It can help you feel more secure in your job, reduce anxiety, and increase your confidence.

It's important to remember that taking action doesn't always mean taking giant leaps. Small, achievable actions can be just as effective in helping you feel more in control and in helping you overcome overthinking your job. For example, you can set small goals for yourself, such as completing a task on time, learning one chapter from your new course, or scheduling a meeting with your supervisor to discuss your performance. These small steps can increase over time and help you achieve your larger goals.

Pause for a second and question yourself gently, *"Are my fears based on facts, or are they being fueled by my overthinking?"*

6

EMBRACE UNCERTAINTY: MAKING PEACE WITH THE UNKNOWN

"The desire for certainty is the root of suffering. Life is uncertain by nature, and resisting it only amplifies fear."

— *Unknown*

One of the strongest fuel sources of overthinking is intolerance of uncertainty. Overthinkers are not necessarily trying to find answers; they are trying to eliminate uncertainty. In fact, the mind falsely believes that if it can predict every outcome, analyze every possibility, and prepare for every scenario, it will feel safe. However, this false sense of control only strengthens anxiety and mental exhaustion.

Human life is inherently uncertain. No amount of thinking can guarantee perfect outcomes, eliminate mistakes, or ensure absolute security. Yet, the overthinking mind refuses to accept this reality. Instead, it engages in compulsive analysis, reassurance-seeking, and mental rehearsals—attempts to gain certainty in an unpredictable world. Ironically, the more one tries to control uncertainty through thinking, the more anxious and overwhelmed one becomes.

Pause for a second and question yourself gently, *"Am I responding to reality as it is, or am I trying to eliminate uncertainty through thinking?"*

Why does uncertainty feel threatening?

From an evolutionary perspective, the primary job of the brain is to detect potential threats and anticipate danger. When the future feels unclear, the mind interprets uncertainty as a risk, activating the fear response. Overthinkers tend to overestimate danger and underestimate their ability to cope, leading to excessive mental planning and rumination.

Common beliefs that maintain overthinking include:

- *"If I don't think this through, something bad will happen."*
- *"I must be certain before I act."*
- *"Uncertainty means loss of control."*

These irrational beliefs trap individuals in a loop where thinking becomes a safety behavior rather than a problem-solving tool.

THE PARADOX OF CONTROL

The truth is simple yet uncomfortable: **certainty is an illusion**. You can control your effort, intentions, and actions—but never outcomes entirely. Life unfolds moment by moment, shaped by countless variables beyond your control. When you resist this reality, the mind stays restless. When you accept it, mental flexibility begins to develop—your ability to adapt to uncertainty is one of the strongest protectors against chronic overthinking.

Embracing uncertainty does not mean being careless or passive. It means acknowledging what is within your control and letting go of what is not (*remember, when you shift or redirect your attention to things you can control or take action on—rather than focusing on what is beyond your control—you begin to shift your paradigm*).

SHIFTING FROM RESISTANCE TO ACCEPTANCE

Acceptance is not resignation; it is clarity. When you accept uncertainty, you stop fighting reality and begin conserving mental energy. Instead of asking, "*What if something goes wrong?*" you start asking, "*If something goes wrong, can I handle it?*" This shift moves you from fear-based thinking to resilience-based thinking. (*Overthinkers are usually more thinking-oriented than action-oriented.*)

A PRACTICAL EXERCISE: THE "UNCERTAINTY PRACTICE"

1. **Notice the urge for certainty:** when you catch yourself overthinking, ask gently, "*Am I trying to eliminate uncertainty right now?*"
2. **Label it clearly:** Silently say, "*This is my discomfort with uncertainty, not a real threat.*"
3. **Allow uncertainty to exist:** Instead of mentally solving the problem, practice sitting with the discomfort for a few minutes. Observe the sensations in your body without reacting.
4. **Refocus on the present action:** Ask, "*What is the next small, practical step I can take right now?*" *Take* action without waiting for perfect clarity.

Each time you allow uncertainty without engaging in overthinking, you strengthen the part of your brain involved in emotional regulation rather than overanalysis. Over time, your tolerance for uncertainty increases, and the urge to overanalyze gradually weakens.

UNCERTAINTY AS A GATEWAY TO GROWTH

Growth, creativity, love, and transformation all exist in the unknown. If life were entirely predictable, there would be no learning, no curiosity, and no evolution.

By embracing uncertainty, you open yourself to new experiences rather than remaining imprisoned by fear.

OVERTHINKING is fueled by the need for certainty, whereas ACCEPTANCE of the unknown or uncertainty cultivates peace.

A powerful reframe is this:

Uncertainty is not danger—it is simply information that has not yet arrived. You don't need to have everything figured out to move forward. You only need the courage to take the next step.

7

THE POWER OF NOW

"If you are not living this moment, you are not really living," says *Eckhart Tolle.*

Overthinking is a common mental challenge that many people struggle with, often finding it difficult to break free from its cycle. However, there are effective ways to overcome it, and one of the most powerful methods is training the mind to remain in the present moment. Learning to live in the present can significantly reduce overthinking and help cultivate a more peaceful and fulfilling life.

Scientific research shows that people who struggle with overthinking spend very little time fully engaged in the present moment. Instead, their minds are often occupied with reliving past experiences or anticipating future outcomes, which later becomes an automatic mental habit. I understand staying anchored in the present may feel challenging, as the mind naturally drifts toward the past or worries about the future. However, by consciously bringing your attention back to the present each time your mind wanders, you gradually train yourself to break free from the habit of overthinking.

One of the most effective steps in managing overthinking is practicing presence through mindful breathing—focusing on your inhale and exhale. This technique is simple yet powerful. Paying attention to your breath anchors you in the present moment and helps calm both the mind and body. To practice this, find a quiet place to sit, close your eyes, and gently focus on your breathing. Take slow, deep breaths and notice the sensation of air moving in and out of your body. As this practice deepens, you become more aware of your thoughts and emotions, allowing you to observe them without getting caught up in them. Practicing this exercise at least three times a day can lead to noticeable improvements in your thought patterns.

In addition to breathing practices, engaging in physical activities can help you stay present. Activities that require full concentration—such as yoga, working out at the gym, swimming, or playing a sport—can enhance focus and rejuvenate the mind. You may also incorporate mindfulness practices, as discussed earlier in this book, to further strengthen your ability to remain grounded in the present moment.

One of the biggest challenges to staying present in today's technological era is constant distraction. You are continuously bombarded with information from phones, computers, and television, making sustained focus difficult. One effective way to counter these distractions is by setting aside dedicated time each day to disconnect. This may be as simple as turning off your phone for an hour or as intentional as taking a short digital detox. By stepping away from technology, you allow your mind to relax and fully engage with the present moment.

It is also important to recognize that being present is a skill that takes time and practice to develop. Do not be hard on yourself when your mind wanders. Instead, gently guide your attention back to the present and continue practicing. Over time, you will find it easier to remain present, and overthinking will gradually lose its grip. When you are fully present, you cannot remain caught in a thinking mode.

In conclusion, cultivating present-moment awareness is a powerful way to overcome overthinking. By training yourself to focus on what is happening right now, you can break free from constant mental analysis and reduce stress. I am asking you to be fully engaged in everyday activities—whether eating, walking, or having a conversation—which allows you to experience life more deeply and meaningfully. For example, focusing on the taste, texture, and aroma of your food helps anchor you in the present rather than allowing your mind to wander.

As discussed, there are many effective ways to cultivate present-moment awareness, including meditation, physical activity, disconnecting from technology, and relaxation techniques such as deep breathing exercises. With consistent practice, patience, and perseverance, you can develop this habit and enjoy greater mental clarity and emotional well-being.

ADD-ON POINTS

1. BE ACTION-ORIENTED: To overcome overthinking, it is crucial to adopt an action-oriented mindset. It is not enough to simply read about the techniques and strategies; you must take the initiative to put them into practice to experience remarkable changes in your thought pattern. So it is best to start small. Choose one technique that resonates with you and commit to implementing it regularly. For instance, if journaling is a technique that you find helpful, set aside a few minutes each day to write down your thoughts and feelings. As you begin to see progress, you can gradually incorporate additional techniques into your routine. Taking action will help you build momentum and create positive habits that will benefit you in the long run. Initially, breaking your routine habits may make you feel uncomfortable. Still, if you are consistently committed to taking small steps, eventually, you will reap the results you desire. Change takes time and effort but is achievable with persistence and determination.

2. SELF-CARE: Self-care is an essential component of managing to overthink. When you prioritize your physical and emotional needs, you are better equipped to navigate the challenges of overthinking. A critical aspect of self-care is ensuring that you get enough sleep. Sleep plays a vital role in regulating mood and hormones, so it is essential to establish a consistent sleep routine that allows you to get the rest you need. Another critical element of self-care is maintaining a healthy diet. Food can profoundly impact your mental and emotional states, as your gut is your second brain. Food consumption can affect your emotions, thoughts, and overall cognitive functions. In other words, *"you are what you eat"* holds true regarding our overall health and well-being.

Additionally, engaging in activities that bring you joy can provide a much-needed respite from the stress of overthinking. These activities might include spending time in nature, pursuing a hobby, or connecting with loved ones. Prioritizing self-care helps you manage stress and reduce overthinking.

3. SET HEALTHY BOUNDARIES: Setting healthy boundaries is a key strategy for overcoming overthinking. When you struggle with overthinking, you may feel the need to control everything or have unrealistic expectations of yourself and others. You can ignore these expectations by setting boundaries and focusing on what's important. In your personal life, setting boundaries means being willing to say no to activities or events that do not align with your values or cause you stress. In your professional life, it means setting specific times for work and prioritizing tasks based on importance. By setting healthy boundaries, you can reduce stress, prioritize self-care, and ultimately live a more fulfilling and balanced life.

4. JOURNALING: Journaling, or writing down your worries, is a powerful tool for overcoming overthinking. When you allow your thoughts to circulate endlessly, they can become overwhelming and often lead to negative consequences like insomnia, difficulty concentrating, and memory-related problems. By writing down your worries, you give yourself a safe and structured outlet to express your thoughts and emotions, helping to reduce their impact and increase your sense of control. Journaling also provides a valuable opportunity for self-reflection, allowing you to gain insight into your thought patterns and behavior. As you develop a regular journaling practice, you can start to identify triggers for your overthinking and work towards developing strategies to manage them more effectively.

5. SEEK PROFESSIONAL HELP: When overthinking significantly impacts your daily life, seeking professional help can be an essential step towards overcoming it. A therapist or psychologist can help you identify the root causes of your overthinking and develop practical strategies to manage it more effectively.

Professional help allows you to explore your thoughts and emotions in a safe and supportive environment where you can build resilience and coping skills. A therapist can also help you identify patterns in your thinking that may contribute to overthinking and provide strategies for retraining your mind to think more positively and rationally. Working with a professional can also offer a fresh perspective and new insights. They can objectively assess the situation and provide guidance towards a more effective and fulfilling path forward. With their support, you can gain a deeper understanding of yourself, develop new skills, and ultimately overcome the challenges of overthinking.

Positive Psychology for a Positive Life

Swathi's Journey from Overthinking to Inner Strength

My Story—In Swathi's Words

My name is Swathi. I'm 26, and I work as a content moderator in Hyderabad. I've always been the quiet, sincere girl—the one who tries to keep everyone happy. On the outside, you would say my life was sorted. But inside my mind, it was a totally different story.

I was an overthinker.

Every small decision—what to wear, how to reply to a message—would end up as a mental marathon in my head. I'd analyze every conversation, predict worst-case scenarios, and fall into an endless pit of "what ifs." Nights were the hardest. Lying in the dark, unable to sleep, my mind would run wild when all I wanted was rest.

If a friend didn't reply quickly, I'd worry I'd done something wrong. Slowly, I started withdrawing—canceling plans, keeping to myself, and avoiding opening up to anyone. I kept a calm face, but deep inside, I was constantly battling a storm.

Things hit a breaking point after I had a mild panic episode at work. Sitting alone in my room that night, exhausted and lost, I decided something had to change. I opened Instagram, searched for psychologists, and scrolled through profiles, and I found an ID—Ram_Prudhvi_Teja (Psychologist). Gathering all my courage, I sent a simple message saying, "*I think I need help. I'm always trapped inside my thoughts.*"

He replied warmly and offered to book an appointment.

Our First Counselling Session:

During our first video session, my voice was barely above a whisper, and my words were clumsy. But I felt comforted when he didn't rush or judge. "*You took the bravest step by reaching out,*" he told me, and for the first time, I felt genuinely understood.

Our sessions slowly became a safe space for me. There was no pressure to pretend. No judgment. Just space—to breathe, to speak, to cry, and sometimes, to just sit in silence. He helped me understand something that shifted everything for me: *that overthinking wasn't a personality flaw. It was just a mental habit*—one that I had unknowingly repeated over the years until it became automatic.

In the following session, he introduced me to something called **mindfulness**. Not as a technique, but as a way of being. "*It's not about stopping your thoughts,*" he said. "*It's about noticing them—without letting them take over.*" At first, it sounded impossible. But I trusted the process.

I started small—just five minutes of walking meditation in my apartment complex. The first few days were awkward. My mind kept wandering. I kept thinking, *"Am I doing this right?"* But gradually, as I focused on the feeling of my breath, the rhythm of my steps, and noticing my physical sensations. Something shifted. I wasn't escaping my thoughts, but I wasn't drowning in them either. For the first time, I began to feel a sense of quiet within.

In the next sessions, he suggested journaling. I started writing every evening. At first, my entries were chaotic—filled with worries, doubts, guilt, and everything I was too scared to say out loud. But slowly, as I wrote more, I started to see patterns in my thinking. The assumptions I made, the old fears I carried, the way I believed every anxious thought as if it were true. It was like holding up a mirror to my mind.

I slowly began learning how to challenge my thoughts—something I had never really done before. For the longest time, I believed that whatever my mind told me was true. If a thought said, *"You're not good enough" or "You'll mess this up,"* I believed it without question. But in one of our sessions, he said something so simple yet powerful:

"Not all thoughts are facts."

I started replacing thoughts like *"I'll definitely mess this up" with "Wait, I've managed things before—I can handle this too."* It wasn't easy, but it felt like slowly reprogramming my inner voice. My mind was no longer my enemy—it was slowly becoming a space I could understand.

Some sessions went deeper than I expected. I found myself opening up about things I hadn't even admitted to myself—old memories, unrealistic expectations I carried, and the guilt I never addressed. I cried more than I thought I would. But Ram never rushed me. He just listened, allowing me to feel whatever came up. During one of those sessions, Ram introduced me to a **forgiveness exercise**—something that helped me begin releasing the emotional burden I had been carrying for years. That night, after our session, I sat on my bed, closed my eyes, and softly started practicing a forgiveness exercise—not just to those who had hurt me, but to **myself** too.

With every passing week, I could feel the shift within me.

My transformation was becoming visible.

How My Life Began to Change

Week after week, small changes began to appear.

- I started sleeping better.
- I raised my hand in meetings without endless mental rehearsals.
- I said "yes" to friends' plans without overanalyzing.
- One day, I laughed wholeheartedly at a silly joke and realized I hadn't done that in months.

My relationships have improved. I was more present and less fearful of others' judgments. My mother noticed the difference, too. "*You look lighter*," she told me one quiet evening over tea.

She was right. My thoughts didn't vanish, but they no longer ran my life. I had learned to live with them instead of being trapped beneath them.

I'll never forget a note I wrote to myself after coming back from a solo trip to Araku Valley:

> *Today, I felt peace in silence.*
>
> *I didn't check my phone every few minutes.*
>
> *I didn't replay old conversations.*
>
> *I just… lived the moment.*

And I smiled, truly and deeply.

A Letter from Me to You

Dear reader,

If you're someone who thinks, worries, and doubts yourself constantly—trust me, you are not alone. For the longest time, I thought there was something "wrong" with me. But reaching out for help and working on myself has changed everything.

Ram didn't just help me "control" my thoughts. He helped me understand myself, heal old wounds, and rediscover small joys again. Now, I know thoughts are like passing clouds; I don't need to fight them. I just need to watch them float by.

Take that first step, even if you're scared or unsure. Healing isn't instant, but it is real.

With love,

Swathi

Swathi's journey is not a miracle. It reflects what many of us experience in silence, carrying invisible burdens. With kindness, the right guidance, and steady effort, even the busiest mind can find stillness and joy again.

21-Day Program to Overcome Overthinking & Regain Mental Clarity

Goal: If you dedicate just 15–30 minutes a day for the next 21 days, you can begin to transform your inner self. This program is designed to reduce overthinking by building awareness, calming the mind, and correcting unhelpful thought patterns—without forcing change. Each day requires only 15–30 minutes. Remember, consistency matters more than intensity.

WEEK 1 – AWARENESS & INTERRUPTING THE CYCLE

Goal: *Notice overthinking instead of fighting it*

Day 1 – Awareness Check

Practice: *Set 3 reminders in the day.*

- *Ask, "What am I thinking right now?"*

Write one recurring thought at night.

Day 2 – Identify Your Enemy

Practice: *Label your dominant pattern:*

- *Worry about the future.*
- *Regret about past*
- *Fear of judgment*

Write: *"My overthinking usually starts when…"*

Day 3 – Thought vs Fact

Practice: *Whenever a thought arises, ask, "**Is this a fact or a thought?**"*

Write 3 thoughts for the day.

Day 4 – Mindfulness exercise for 5 minutes

Practice:

- *Sit quietly for 5 minutes.*
- *Focus on breath.*
- *Let thoughts pass without engagement.*

No forcing. Just observing.

Day 5 – Walking Meditation

Practice:

- *Walk slowly for 10 minutes.*
- *Focus only on steps and breathing.*

If the mind wanders, gently return.

Day 6 – Stop the Loop

Practice: *When overthinking starts, say internally,* ***"Not now."***

Shift attention to body sensation (feet, breath).

Day 7 – Reflection Day

Reflect*:*

- *What patterns am I repeating every day?*
- *When is overthinking becoming overwhelmed?*

Write one insight.

____

____

____

____

____

____

____

____

____

____

If overthinking still shows up, remember this: it does not mean failure—it means your brain is unlearning old patterns. Healing is not linear. Stay consistent, stay curious, and move forward with compassion toward yourself.

WEEK 2 – CORRECTING THINKING ERRORS

Goal: *Reduce the emotional intensity of thoughts*

Day 8 – Spot Thinking Errors

Practice: *Identify one or two thinking errors today:*

- *Catastrophizing*
- *Mind reading*
- *All-or-nothing thinking*

Day 9 – Socratic Questioning

Practice (write answers):

- *What evidence supports this thought?*
- *What evidence goes against it?*

Day 10 – Alternative Thought

Practice:

- *Replace one irrational thought with a balanced one.*
- *Example: "I will fail." → "I may struggle, but I can learn."*

Day 11 – Director Technique

Practice:

- *Imagine thoughts as scenes in a movie.*
- *Watch without reacting for 5 minutes.*

Day 12 – Emotional Distance

Practice: *Throughout the day, whenever a distressing or repetitive thought arises, gently say to yourself:*

- ***"I am having the thought that…"*** *and then complete the sentence with the thought you noticed.*
- *Example: Instead of "Nobody understands me," say, "I am having the thought that nobody understands me."*

This creates psychological distance.

Day 13 – Journaling for Clarity

- *Write freely for 10 minutes: No correction and no judgment*
- *End with one calm statement.*

Day 14 – Weekly Reset

Reflect:

- *Is overthinking intensity reduced?*
- *Which tool works best for you?*

____

____

____

By completing Week 2, you have already taken back more control than you may realize. Overthinking does not disappear overnight, but awareness weakens its grip. Each time you pause, observe, and choose differently, you are training your mind toward clarity. Continue with patience—your mind is learning a new way to be.

WEEK 3 – LETTING GO & BUILDING A NEW MINDSET

Goal: *Release past, build trust, strengthen calmness within*

Day 15 – Clean the Past

Practice:

- *Identify one past memory you replay often.*
- *Write what it taught you.*

Day 16 – Reframing Exercise

Practice: *Change the meaning of the past event:*

- *From pain → learning*
- *From failure → growth*

Day 17 – Forgiveness Practice

Practice: *Close your eyes and say silently,* ***"I forgive myself. I release this."***

Day 18 – Control vs Acceptance

Practice:

List:

- *What is in my control*
- *What is not*
- *Drop what is not.*

Day 19 – Trust the Present

Practice: *For today, decide,* ***"I will handle things when they happen."***

Day 20 – Mental Diet

Practice:

- *Avoid: Over-analysis and excess reassurance seeking (Important)*

Choose one grounding activity.

Day 21 – Integration Day

Reflect:

- *How has my relationship with thoughts changed?*
- *Write a commitment for the next 30 days.*

____

____

____

____

____

____

____

____

____

____

Key Reminders for all 21 days:

- *Do not fight with thoughts*
- *Do not judge yourself*
- *Do not aim for perfection*
- *Aim for* **awareness and consistency.**

Author's Note:

Overthinking does not disappear suddenly. It ***loses power slowly*** *when you stop feeding it. Always remember, YOU CAN DO THIS.*

SUMMARY

This book focuses on self-improvement and personal growth by identifying and addressing destructive thought patterns. The first step in this journey is recognizing and becoming aware of these patterns. The book emphasizes mindfulness practices, mainly walking meditation, to cultivate this awareness. It also explores cognitive distortions—common thinking patterns contributing to negative emotions and behaviors. Individuals can enhance their mental well-being by recognizing and challenging these distortions. Another key concept discussed is becoming an observer of one's thoughts, which involves stepping back and noticing thoughts and emotions without judgment. This practice helps individuals avoid negative thought patterns and gain a clearer perspective.

This book also emphasizes the importance of letting go of past experiences and not allowing them to define one's present or future. It addresses the fears underlying overthinking and offers practical techniques to help individuals break free from this habit. In addition, the book explores how embracing uncertainty, living in the present, and practicing mindfulness can lead to inner peace and happiness. The practice of being fully present in the moment is presented as a powerful tool for personal growth and overall well-being.

CONCLUSION

As we reach the end of this book, I want to express my gratitude for taking the time to read it. Your dedication and enthusiasm for self-improvement are truly admirable. Learning is the first step toward personal growth, and you have done an outstanding job. However, personal transformation goes beyond simply acquiring knowledge—it requires action. As the saying goes, **"Knowing is different from doing,"** which holds true in every aspect of life. No self-help book or motivational seminar can create lasting change unless you decide to take ACTION. I encourage you to take small, consistent steps toward a more positive life. Even the most minor actions can create a profound impact over time. Have faith in yourself, visualize your desired future, and let these positive images guide and motivate you.

Always remember that success is a journey, not a destination. It requires patience, perseverance, and consistent effort. Growth takes time, and every small step brings you closer to becoming the best version of yourself. Believe in yourself and your ability to achieve greatness. You have the strength, wisdom, and resilience to create your desired life. So, take that leap of faith and start your journey toward a more positive and fulfilling life today!

I'll end by emphasizing that you cannot continue thinking, feeling, and acting as you did yesterday and expect different or better results. It's neither possible nor practical. If you want positive changes, you must take responsibility for your thoughts, feelings, and actions and consciously shift them in a positive direction. You can change your life and create the reality you desire.

It's important to understand that you are the author of your life, and your choices determine its direction and quality. Breaking old habits and thought patterns may be challenging, but it is not impossible.

Always remember that you are the creator of your life, and you have the potential to shape it in any direction you choose. You can create a meaningful, fulfilling, and joyful life by taking charge of your thoughts, emotions, and actions and consistently making positive choices.

About the Author

Ram Prudhvi Teja is a psychologist, author, and mind–body therapist. He is also a certified Cognitive Behavioral Therapy (CBT) practitioner. Born and raised in Kovvur, a small town in Andhra Pradesh, he completed his master's degree in psychology at Acharya Nagarjuna University and holds a postgraduate diploma in mental health.

Alongside his professional pursuits, Ram is an avid reader who enjoys exploring a wide range of genres, from romance to psychology. He is deeply passionate about transforming lives and has dedicated himself to offering counselling, training, and coaching services that empower individuals to lead more positive and healthy lives. An ardent traveler, he loves discovering new places and immersing himself in diverse cultures. His interactions with people from varied backgrounds have enriched his understanding of human behavior—insights that are reflected in his writing. Drawing inspiration from real-life experiences, he brings depth and relatability to his work.

Ram strongly believes in the transformative power of words. His commitment to making a difference in people's lives fuels his writing, with the goal of inspiring readers to become the best versions of themselves.

If you would like to get in touch with Ram Prudhvi Teja, he can be reached at ramprudhviteja.psychologist@gmail.com, or you can follow him on Instagram @ram_prudhvi_teja.

www.ingramcontent.com/pod-product-compliance
Lightning Source LLC
La Vergne TN
LVHW090332210926
848480LV00004B/1378